WRITE YOUR OWN

HISTORICAL FICTION

STORY

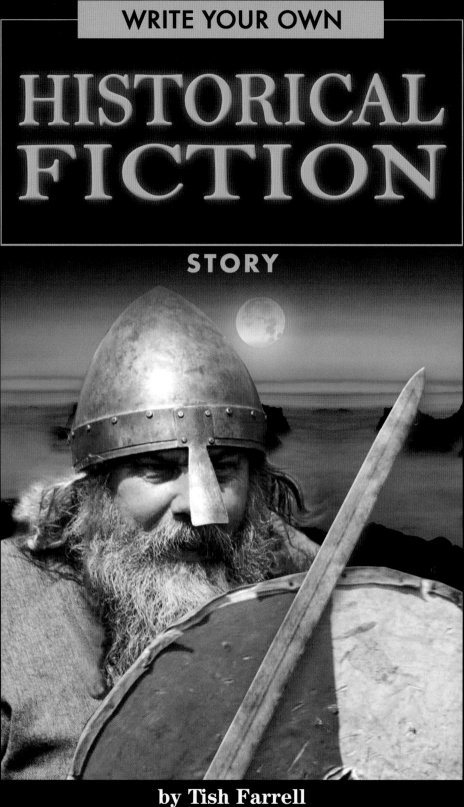

by Tish Farrell

First published in the United States in 2006 by
Compass Point Books
3109 West 50th Street #115
Minneapolis, MN 55410

Copyright © ticktock Entertainment Ltd 2006
First published in Great Britain in 2006 by ticktock Media Ltd.,
ISBN 1 86007 532 0 PB
A CIP catalogue record for this book is available from the British Library.

Visit Compass Point Books on the Internet at
www.compasspointbooks.com
or email your request to
custserv@compasspointbooks.com

For Compass Point Books
Sue Vander Hook, Nick Healy, Anthony Wacholtz, Nathan Gassman, James Mackey,
Abbey Fitzgerald, Catherine Neitge, Keith Griffin, and Carol Jones

For ticktock Entertainment Ltd
Graham Rich, Elaine Wilkinson, John Lingham,
Suzy Kelly, Heather Scott, Jeremy Smith

Library of Congress Cataloging-in-Publication Data
Farrell, Tish.
  Write your own historical fiction story / by Tish Farrell.
     p. cm.—(Write your own)
  Includes bibliographical references and index.
  Audience: Grade 4-6.
  ISBN 0-7565-1640-4 (hard cover)
  1. Historical fiction—Authorship—Juvenile literature. I. Title. II. Series.
PN3377.5.H57F37 2006
808.3'81—dc22   2005030729

Your writing journey

Do you have a passion for the past? If you long to bring historical events to life in your own stories, this book will show you how. You will learn to write your own historical fiction, which lets characters from your imagination encounter real people and events from the past. Your stories can have a sort of energy not found in history books. Now get ready to fire up your time machine and journey back in time.

CONTENTS

WANT TO BE A WRITER?

This book is the perfect place to start. It aims to give you the tools to write your own historical fiction. Learn how to craft believable characters and perfect plots with satisfying beginnings, middles, and endings. Examples from famous books appear throughout, with tips and techniques from published authors to help you on your way.

Get the writing habit

Do timed and regular practice. Real writers learn to write even when they don't particularly feel like it.

Create a story-writing zone.

Keep a journal.

Keep a notebook—record interesting events and note how people behave and speak.

Generate ideas

Find a character whose story you want to tell. What is his or her problem?

Brainstorm to find out everything about your character.

Research settings, events, and other characters.

Get a mix of good and evil characters.

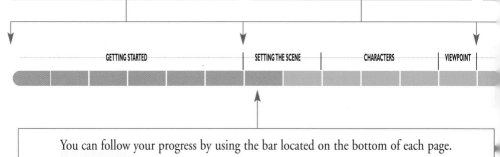

GETTING STARTED · SETTING THE SCENE · CHARACTERS · VIEWPOINT

You can follow your progress by using the bar located on the bottom of each page. The orange color tells you how far along the story-writing process you have gotten. As the blocks are filled out, your story will be growing.

Plan

What is your story about?

What happens?

Plan beginning, middle, and end.

Write a synopsis or create story-boards.

Write

Write the first draft, then put it aside for a while.

Check spelling and dialogue—does it flow?

Remove unnecessary words.

Does the story have a good title and satisfying ending?

Avoid clichés.

Publish

Write or print the final draft.

Always keep a copy for yourself.

Send your story to children's magazines, Internet writing sites, competitions, or school magazines.

SYNOPSES AND PLOTS   WINNING WORDS   SCINTILLATING SPEECH   HINTS AND TIPS   THE NEXT STEP

When you get to the end of the bar, your book is ready to go! You are an author!
You now need to decide what to do with your book and what your next project should be.
Perhaps it will be a sequel to your story, or maybe something completely different.

BEGIN YOUR BLAST TO THE PAST

Historical-story writers transport their readers back in time by the power of their words. The first thing you need to do to succeed is gather your writing materials and find a good place to work. All you need is a pen and paper. A computer can make writing quicker, but it is not essential.

What you need

As a historical-fiction writer you'll need to delve into the past—at your local museum, library, or on the Internet. To help organize your findings, you may find the following useful:

- a small notebook that you carry everywhere
- plenty of scrap paper for writing practice
- pencils and pens for drawing ancient maps and timelines
- Post-it notes to mark reference book pages
- stick-on stars for highlighting key information in your research notes
- files to keep your fact-finding organized and story ideas safe

- index cards for recording key facts
- dictionary, thesaurus, and encyclopedia
- a good general history book to check basic facts
- a camera to record any historic sites you visit

Your writing place

Writers can work where they choose. Some have writing cottages or home offices with lots of inspiring objects around them. Some work in basements; others work in public places, like coffee shops. Experiment. Find somewhere comfortable—perhaps your bedroom or the library. Perhaps your local museum has just the right creative feeling.

Create a story-writing zone

- Play music from your favorite historical period.
- Have some historical images laid out around you.
- Put on a hat that you only wear when you're writing (make one or adapt one you already have).
- Choose intriguing objects for your desk—an old family photograph, a war medal, a shard of ancient pottery, an arrowhead— anything that has a story to tell.

Writer's golden rule

Once you have chosen your writing space, the first step in becoming a writer is: Go there as often as possible and write. You must write and write regularly. This is the writer's golden rule.

Until you are sitting at your desk with pen in hand, no writing can happen. It doesn't matter what you write—an e-mail or a diary entry will do— as long as you write something.

Before you can bring the past to life in historical fiction, you must get into training. The best writers practice writing every day, even when they don't feel inspired. So train as you would to be an athlete!

Now it's your turn

Great events

Sit at your desk, close your eyes, and take four deep breaths. Now open your eyes and write "The Boston Tea Party" at the top of the page. Then brainstorm. See how many other historical events, phrases, and names you can scribble down in two minutes. Write every thought that comes to mind.

TIPS AND TECHNIQUES

Despite a peasants' revolt or the fall of Rome, keep your date with your desk. Even two minutes' practice a day is better than none.

Now it's your turn

A slice of time

Think about your favorite historical event (you probably mentioned it in the brainstorming exercise on page 8). Imagine a time machine has taken you back there. Close your eyes and try to visualize it. What can you feel, hear, smell, touch, and see? Take 10 minutes to write down all your first thoughts. Don't worry about writing complete sentences. Scribble down every impression, even if it seems silly. This is about becoming a writer, not about being the best writer.

When you've finished, give yourself a gold star. You have unlocked your long-lost story archive. The more you do this, the easier it will be to overcome the Story Executioner— your internal critic that always finds fault with your writing.

Case study

In 1930, Laura Ingalls Wilder couldn't find a publisher for her autobiography **Pioneer Girl**, so she used parts of it to create the first of the much-loved Little House books—**Little House in the Big Woods**. This story is based on Laura's pioneering life in the big woods of Wisconsin during the late 19th century. Because the writer changed some of the facts, it is called historical fiction rather than autobiography.

Mark Twain and Charles Dickens (left) were not historical-fiction writers. They wrote about their own times. But their books may help you "tune in" to the ways people thought, talked, and lived in the past.

Your own historical fiction

You can bring the past to life through characters created in your own imagination. Historical fiction usually blends facts about the past with imagined stories and characters. Your characters—whether they are gladiators engaged in brutal battles, pioneer children facing the struggles of the frontier, or innocent people forced into prison camps during World War II—can encounter real people and events from the past. But in historical fiction the outcome is uncertain until the story's ending, creating a sort of drama and energy not found in history books.

Read, read, read!

Reading will help you decide which period you most want to write about and should spark ideas. Jot them down in a notebook.

Now it's your turn

Gaining inspiration

Reread your favorite historical-fiction novel. Imagine you are writing it. Look at how the writer uses specific historical details to bring the past to life. Make notes on your thoughts. Copy down one or two of your favorite passages. Underline the details that make a scene work. Try to sketch out what you are reading. Ask yourself if you understand the scene better by drawing it. Did it give you any new ideas about what was happening?

Case study

Joseph Bruchac writes historical novels that show the important place of Native Americans in American history. Much of his writing draws on his Abenaki ancestry. His American Indian heritage is just one part of an ethnic background that includes Slovak and English blood, but it is the element that has shaped his life the most.

Make notes

Grow your imagination. But if you are not enjoying a book, leave it and start another. Make a note of why you didn't like it. You might find this information useful later. Read some nonfiction history books, too.

TIPS AND TECHNIQUES

As you read, think about whose story you want to tell. In which time and place do the characters live? Record all ideas in your notebook so you will have plenty to draw from for your own story.

FIND YOUR VOICE

Reading lots of good books will help you discover your own writer's voice, which is your own style of writing. It takes most writers a long time to develop their own unique voice.

A writer's voice

Once you start reading as a would-be writer, you'll see that writers have their own rhythm and range of language that stays the same throughout the book. Karen Cushman (*Catherine, Called Birdy*) writes quite differently from Harry Mazer (*A Boy at War*), and Kevin Crossley-Holland (*The Seeing Stone*) writes nothing like Michael Cadnum (*The Leopard Sword*), even though they both write about people going to war in the Middle Ages.

Historic voices

As a writer of historical stories, don't be tempted to use old-fashioned language. Readers quickly tire of too many unfamiliar words. Instead, occasionally use terms from the period, such as personal greetings, to suggest a particular time.

Experiment

For storytelling ideas, try reading other genres. Caroline Lawrence (The Roman Mysteries series) sets her detective stories in ancient Rome. Legends might inspire you, too, as they did Kevin Crossley-Holland in the Arthur series.

WRITERS' VOICES

Look at the following extracts. Not all of them use old-fashioned phrasing, but can you spot the verbal clues the others use to suggest a past time?

1665, Derbyshire, England

A parcel of patterns brought the Plague to Eyam. A parcel sent up from London to George Vicars, a journeyman tailor. ... This was the common report and credence amongst us, though I heard later that the Plague was at Derby at the time when it reached us.

Jill Paton Walsh, *A Parcel of Patterns*

1850s, Mississippi

Julilly ached with tiredness and hunger gnawed wildly at her stomach. ... The other slave girls along the floor slept heavily, but Liza was restless.

"You is a friend," the crippled girl whispered. "No one else ever picked the high cotton that my poor ol' back won't stretch to."

Barbara Smucker, *Runaway to Freedom*

1870s, Missouri

Well, I catched my breath and most fainted. Shut up on a wreck with such a gang as that! But it warn't no time to be sentimentering. We'd got to find that boat now-had to have it for ourselves.

Mark Twain, *Huckleberry Finn*

World War II, England

When Chas awakened, the air-raid shelter was silent. Grey winter light was creeping round the door-curtain. It could have been any time. His mother was gone, and the little brown attaché case with the insurance policies and bottle of brandy for emergencies. The all-clear must have gone.

Robert Westall, *The Machine Gunners*

To write historical fiction, you must be a good storyteller and a determined history detective. It may help to start by writing a story set during a time period you have studied at school.

Start from what you know

Look through your past school assignments—maybe having to do with the ancient Egyptians or the Middle Ages. Start looking for your hero. Search for a dilemma. What is happening in your character's world that is causing big problems?

How one writer found her story

Patricia Curtis Pfitsch says the idea for *Riding the Flume* came from reading a nonfiction book about sequoia trees. The controversial cutting of the trees was just the sort of conflict a storyteller needs. Out of her research into the issue grew the character Francie. This is part of the plot summary from the book's back cover:

> *During the summer of 1894, the giant sequoia trees— the oldest living things on earth—are being felled for lumber in northern California. Francie finds a note in a hole of an old sequoia stump and recognizes her sister's handwriting. But Carrie died in an accident six years earlier. Could the secret still be important? Francie is determined to find out.*
> from *Riding the Flume* by Patricia Curtis Pfitsch

Now it's your turn

Turn fact to fiction

You are in a plague-ridden city of the mid-1600s. The sick are locked in their houses. Men with carts collect the dead. Dogcatchers round up stray animals. Pretend you are a lost spaniel. How do you survive on the streets? How do you escape the dogcatcher? For historical details, read Kathryn Hinds' *Life in the Middle Ages: The City.*

Research is not the full story

Historical research gives you details of places, events, and human conflicts. The historical-fiction writer's art is to shape them into a gripping personal story. For example, in *Riding the Flume,* the main story isn't about cutting sequoias. It is about Francie and her reaction to the tree cutting.

Readers are involved with her dilemmas. They want to know how she will save some of the sequoias, how she will solve the mystery of her dead sister, and if she will have the courage to ride the flume. The research helps writers to create a believable and exciting tale.

The home front

Many historical-story writers start out by basing their stories on their own family's history. Quiz older family members for their memories. There may be old photo albums, wills, family recipes, or letters. This evidence from your own family's past may "speak" to you in surprising ways.

Back to basics

Go back to the exercise you did on page 9, writing down your thoughts about a historical event. Did you have any problems—details you didn't know about dress, transport, or the way of life? Perhaps you put in things that hadn't been invented yet—a wristwatch, a skateboard, or a computer? This is easily done, so don't worry.

Case study

Mildred D. Taylor (Roll of Thunder, Hear My Cry) was born in Mississippi, the great-granddaughter of a white plantation owner and a slave. She grew up listening to her father's stories about slavery. Years later, when she was trying to tell her grandmother's story about the felling of trees on their family land, the strong-willed character of Cassie Logan emerged, leading to Mildred's books about the Logan family in 1930s America.

Now it's your turn

Every picture tells a story

Take a break from writing. Capture the past in drawings. Make a scrapbook or collage of everyday life in your chosen historical time. Download images from the Internet or ask the librarian if you can photocopy some pictures from books. Pictures give you something concrete to describe in stories. Visit your museum and draw interesting objects. If you are allowed to touch them, go for it! Find out what it's like to hold an old pistol or turn a butter churn.

Check out facts in your library and museum

Family history is often patchy—people forget things or remember them incorrectly.

So head for the library and ask the librarian what kinds of historical documents you can consult.

• Old newspapers on microfilm can tell you a lot about the way of life.

• Maps and directories show how your town grew.

• Census records note who lived where and how they made a living.

• Church and government records note births, marriages, and deaths.

Organize the facts

Use index cards to record facts and where you found them. Three-ring binders with plastic sleeves are good for storing pictures and newspaper clippings.

CHAPTER 2: SETTING THE SCENE

LIVE IN THE PAST

In historical stories the setting must be accurate, and it must include the time and the place. Don't overload your story with details, however. It's like preparing a stage for a play—just the right props must be there for the actors to perform their parts, but there shouldn't be a lot of extras.

Common experiences

Think about how it feels to visit another country or an unfamiliar part of your own city or state. What do you notice most? Is it the shops and the streets, or the way people talk, dress, and look? Do you notice different food, vehicles, or houses? Readers will be interested in those sorts of details from a past time. Those simple details can make your story seem real.

Now it's your turn

Hysterical history

Take a break from research. Throw facts to the wind. For 10 minutes, brainstorm your ideal past. Choose all your favorite bits of history and mix their clothes, buildings, places, times, transportation, people, and events. Samurai girl meets King Tut? Cool!

Now it's your turn

Start up your time machine!

Imagine you are a tour operator who does guided time-machine trips to your chosen past. Plan your route around your setting. Write a few paragraphs about it. Sketch the tour highlights of your created historical world—maybe it's a trip up the Nile in a papyrus reed boat, a look inside a medicine man's home, a nighttime walk along the Great Wall of China, or a glimpse of the frontier hangman's noose. Doing this exercise will help you spot gaps in what you know about your own setting.

Create the setting

Once you have researched enough facts, creating the setting is somewhat like doing a jigsaw puzzle. If you choose only the most vivid, interesting details that affect your characters and plot, your readers should be able to fill in the rest of the picture.

TIPS AND TECHNIQUES

Step into your characters' shoes. As you go back in time, differences between rich and poor peoples' lives may be striking. There was far less freedom in every area of life. Values have changed, too. Behavior that we find shocking now might have been acceptable then, and certainly actions we accept today would have been outrageous in many eras of the past.

How will you transport your readers back in time? Consider how to bring the past to life in ways that readers can easily relate to. Show what your characters feel.

Choose an authentic setting

In Jill Paton Walsh's *A Parcel of Patterns*, the simple need to eat shows the historical setting. Eyam villagers are confined to their settlement so they won't spread the plague. Food deliveries to the village boundary chart the plague's course:

> *The Duke sent still the bread and bacon ... to us in ample quantity, soon more by far than the living could eat up. So we took less, and left some lying at the boundary-stones. ... And the sight of the spare loaves lying struck chill into the hearts of the Duke's servants.*
>
> Jill Paton Walsh, *A Parcel of Patterns*

TIPS AND TECHNIQUES

Show historical situations from the main character's viewpoints. Make them personal. Be specific—the dead rat stink in the dungeon or the roast hog juices dribbling down a hero's chin.

Now it's your turn

Ace adjectives

Read the quote on page 20 aloud. Notice how the verbs and adjectives bring the place to life. Now write a scene from your story. Show your hero scaling a wall, pushing through a market, or running away. Use his or her movement through a specific place to create the setting.

Add some action

Mesh the setting with some quick action. In V.A. Richardson's *The House of Windjammer*, it is 1636. The hero, Adam, is dashing through Amsterdam's streets, late for his meeting with his tutor.

He cut up between the warehouses and into the squeeze of the alleys and streets. Here the streets burrowed between top-heavy houses that sagged under the weight of their upper floors and roofs. At every turn more streets and alleys opened to the left and right, filled with smoke of fires and the belch of pewter factories. Through the maze of sounds and smells ... he picked his way until he ran straight into trouble.
V.A. Richardson, *The House of Windjammer*

DISCOVER YOUR HERO

When creating your characters, you must start with the historical facts. Your protagonist, or hero, will be shaped by the times he or she lives in, just as you are. But to make a good story, the character must challenge the system in some way.

Build character

Once you know your hero's problems, you can start shaping him or her into a real person. Regard your hero as a new friend. Ask what he or she wants for a better life. How will he or she get it? What if he or she fails? Find out your hero's likes and dislikes. What are his or her strengths and weaknesses? Can they add drama to the story?

Find a good name

Names come in and out of fashion, so take care. Your Victorian maid won't be called Kylie. Biblical names like Jacob or Job were common in the past. Graveyards and old newspapers are good places to look. Once you have a name, find ways to make your hero sympathetic. If you don't really like him or her, your readers won't either. This is another reason for giving your hero some flaws. No one likes a perfect person.

Now it's your turn

Rough justice?

Brainstorm about your feelings. For seven minutes, write about how it felt when you were betrayed, bullied, or unfairly accused. Then write for seven minutes from the point of view of the person who hurt you. You now have some raw materials to help you create your characters' feelings.

Give them a past

Even historical heroes need some history, just enough to explain their current situation. In *Stop the Train*, Geraldine McCaughrean briefly describes pioneer Cissie's old life as she thinks of the new life she has ahead. If your hero has a complicated past, it could be told in a flashback scene, in conversation with a friend, or perhaps as a short prologue, which introduces your story.

> *It had to be better than the filthy rooming-house they had left behind in Arkansas, with its rats in the basement and flies in the milk.*
>
> Geraldine McCaughrean, *Stop the Train*

Decide what they look like

In real life, people don't often describe themselves directly, so if your hero is your narrator, you may have to be sly in delivering this information. You could get your hero to describe himself or herself as he or she looks into a mirror or as he or she puts on clothes for a special occasion. Or another character could comment on the hero's appearance in dialogue.

TIPS AND TECHNIQUES

If you can't imagine what your hero looks like, search old pictures or photographs. Find a face that fits your story and describe it.

CREATE YOUR VILLAIN

As you have seen, heroes need problems to solve. These might be caused by human enemies (antagonists), by their own flaws, or by war, slavery, plague, invasion, or poverty.

A bad situation

In 16th-century Venice, only the eldest daughter of a noble household was allowed to marry. If the family was very rich, the second eldest might also. But in Donna Jo Napoli's *Daughter of Venice*, heroine Donata is a second-born twin, and she reflects on the bind she's in:

> *Unless I marry, a convent lies ahead for me, too. I'd die in a convent.*
> Donna Jo Napoli, *Daughter of Venice*

TIPS AND TECHNIQUES

Your villain should be as well thought out as your hero. Don't make villains too obvious. They might even start out as your hero's friend.

Enemies everywhere

In *The House of Windjammer* by V. A. Richardson, Adam Windjammer has many enemies, especially the sinister preacher Abner Heems:

> *Abner Heems was just standing there, his hat pulled down low over his eyes ... his shoulders hunched against the cold. The preacher had come stealing to their door as quiet as Death.*
> V. A. Richardson, *The House of Windjammer*

Picture of cruelty

In Barbara Smucker's *Runaway to Freedom*, Julilly's main "enemy" is her life of slavery, but she also has a human enemy—the slave overseer, Sims:

> *Mama Sally held Julilly close as they walked outside and joined the field-hand line. The man with the jay-bird voice strode back and forth in front of them. ... His cheeks puffed and jiggled as he walked. Julilly noticed that his fingers puffed, too, over the whip that he flicked in his hand.*
> Barbara Smucker, *Runaway to Freedom*

Own worst enemy

In Leon Garfield's *The Empty Sleeve*, Peter Gannet is his own worst enemy. Envy of his twin, Paul, and a burning ambition to run away to sea lead him into a life of dishonesty.

Now it's your turn

Know your villain

Take 10 minutes to brainstorm your hero's human enemy. What does your villain do and what is his or her motivation? Is he or she truly bad or simply a product of the times? Does he or she have weaknesses that will affect the story? Describe what he or she looks like. Draw a picture, too.

DEVELOP A SUPPORTING CAST

The best way to show readers what your hero is really like is to have them interacting with other characters. Minor characters can add drama and complication to the story.

Character sketches

Charles Dickens' books are a good place to learn about creating memorable minor characters. In *Great Expectations*, Pip describes his bullying sister, Mrs. Joe:

> *My sister ... had such a prevailing redness of skin, that I sometimes used to wonder whether it was possible she washed herself with a nutmeg-grater instead of soap.*
> Charles Dickens, *Great Expectations*

Take two

In Geraldine McCaughrean's *Stop the Train*, two mail-order brides step off the Osage stagecoach. From this description, which do you think will be more important to the story?

> *One of the ladies was a slim needle of a woman with plump, pink cheeks, wearing a crushed bonnet and net gloves. The other wore a bright yellow plaid underskirt, her iris-blue overdress caught up behind into a bustle so extravagant that it resembled a bunch of daffodils sprung from a ledge above the sea. A pair of old scarlet riding gloves were tucked into her waistband.*
> Geraldine McCaughrean, *Stop the Train*

Real-life characters

Some historical stories feature real-life figures—often kings and queens. But it's safest to have them only as "walk-on" characters. In *A Northern Light*, for example, Jennifer Donnelly uses the letters of the real Grace Brown, who drowned at Big Moose Lake in July 1906.

Now it's your turn

More character building

For 10 minutes, brainstorm a brief biography of one of your minor characters—a protagonist or an antagonist. Say what the character's role is in your story. Find a few special features that make him or her stand out—a sense of humor, a limp, bright red hair, or something else you imagine. Write your first thoughts only.

Revealing character

In Jennifer Donnelly's *A Northern Light*, the heroine, Mattie, and her friend Weaver Smith's love of words shines out in the "word duels" they play over the word "iniquitous":

> *"Evil!" Weaver yelled.*
> *"Immoral!" I shouted.*
> *"Sinful!"*
> *"Wrong!"*
> *"Unrighteous!"*
> *"Unjust!"*
> *"Wicked!"*
> *"Corrupt!"*
> Jennifer Donnelly,
> *A Northern Light*

CHOOSE A POINT OF VIEW

It is common to tell a historical story from your hero's point of view. This makes the story more personal.

The first person

The first-person point of view (POV) speaks directly to the reader, almost like a letter. For example, "I broke into the castle by swimming the moat" instantly seems more real than "Squire John broke into the castle." It gives your story the ring of truth in a way other viewpoints can't. You can use it to tell your story as a narrative. The disadvantage of this POV is that readers only get to know the other characters through the hero's accounts of them or when the narrator reports others' speech in dialogue.

The third person

With the third-person viewpoint, which uses "he" or "she" rather than "I" to describe the main character, events are described as if viewed from inside your hero's head. Again, readers only know what other characters are thinking if it is reported in dialogue.

> *Carrie saw the marks of their rubber-soled shoes and felt guilty, though it wasn't her fault. Nick whispered, "She thinks we're poor children, too poor to have slippers," and giggled.*
>
> Nina Bawden, *Carrie's War*

GETTING STARTED   SETTING THE SCENE   CHARACTERS   VIEWPOINT

Know all

Another viewpoint is the omniscient—or "all-seeing"—view. It's usually used in traditional stories, and it means that readers can be told everything all characters think and feel. The narrator can even know things the characters don't.

Now it's your turn

A change of view

Write a short scene from your own story. Have your hero doing something with others. Describe the scene as the omniscient narrator—saying what is happening to everyone. Then rewrite it in the third person, from your hero's point of view. Finally, try it in the first person. Which version do you prefer and why?

Mix views

In historical stories, it is quite common to have diary entries and letters included in the narrative. These give you a chance to change viewpoints in a natural way (such as moving from third-person narrative to first-person diary or letter excerpts).

TELL YOUR STORY'S STORY

When your story begins to take shape in your mind, sum up the main theme and plot in a few paragraphs. This is called a synopsis.

On the back covers of historical novels, the "blurb" briefly sets the scene and makes readers want to find out more. A synopsis should do the same. Here are two excerpts from blurbs:

> *It was only after meeting the proud, resourceful Indian boy that Matt began to discover new ways to survive in the forest. And in getting to know his friend, Matt also began to understand the heritage and way of the life of the Beaver clan and their growing problem in adapting to the white man and the changing frontier.*
>
> from *The Sign of the Beaver* by George Speare

> *Why is the land so important to Cassie's family? It takes the events of one turbulent year—the year of the night riders and the burnings, the year a white girl humiliates Cassie in public simply because she is black—to show Cassie that having a place of their own is the Logan family's lifeblood.*
>
> from *Roll of Thunder, Hear My Cry* by Mildred D. Taylor

GETTING STARTED   SETTING THE SCENE   CHARACTERS   VIEWPOINT

Now it's your turn

Hungry readers

Sum up your story in a single striking sentence, then develop it in two or three short paragraphs. Try to whet your readers' appetites. Show where your story is going without giving away the actual ending.

Think about your theme. In most stories, the general theme is the triumph of good over evil. Historical stories might also tackle the abuse of power, overcoming hardship or persecution, righting a wrong, or getting revenge.

Make a story map

You have a synopsis that says what your story is about. You have a cast of characters and a setting. You know from whose viewpoint you wish to tell the tale. The next useful tool is a

story map. Before filmmakers start filming, they map out the plot in a series of sketches or storyboards. This helps them to decide how best to film the story. You can do this for your story. Draw the main episodes in pictures and add a few notes that say what is happening in each scene.

TIPS AND TECHNIQUES

Writing a synopsis can bring unexpected ideas to the surface. If you can't describe your story in a couple of paragraphs, it is too complicated. Simplify it. Keep asking yourself: "Whose story is this and how will I tell it?"

Create a synopsis

Before they start writing their stories, novelists often list all their chapters, outlining what will happen in each one. This is called a chapter synopsis. *The Merry Adventures of Robin Hood* by Howard Pile tells the tales of a famous character in historical fiction. Looking at one Robin Hood story, you can determine the main story points and see how they build on one another to create the full story.

A famous example

Here are storyboard captions for a story in *The Merry Adventures of Robin Hood*:

1. It is the time of Richard I, and the Sheriff of Nottingham sends an outlaw, Guy of Gisbourne, to kill Robin Hood.

2. Robin kills Guy and, disguising himself in Guy's cowl, goes to find the Sheriff.

3. Meanwhile, Little John meets a widow whose sons are to be hanged by the Sheriff.

4. Little John goes in disguise and meets the Sheriff. He agrees to be the hangman.

5. Little John frees the brothers but is captured.

6. As Little John is to be hanged, Robin arrives, dressed as Guy, and says he has killed Robin.

7. For his reward, he asks permission to kill Little John and has him tied to a tree.

8. Robin frees Little John and tells him to pick up the weapons he has hidden in the woods.

9. Robin reveals who he is and draws his bow on the Sheriff.

10. The terrified Sheriff and his men flee for the safety of Nottingham's city gates.

Novels versus short stories

Novels have beginnings, middles, and ends just like short stories, but the stories themselves are more complex. Novels have more details, more character development, and, probably, several subplots. In a larger tale, chapters make the storytelling more manageable. Each one has a beginning, middle, and end, like a mini-story inside the larger one, but it also carries the story forward, adding more mystery and creating more suspense.

Expanding a short story

To make the Robin Hood story into a short novel, you would need to think how each storyboard scene could be expanded to show readers more about the characters, their problems, and the times they lived in. For example, chapter one might start with some historical scene-setting that demonstrates how the Sheriff of Nottingham has gained so much power. If you include a scene with the Sheriff plotting with Guy, this will show readers what kind of villains they are and explain their different reasons for wanting Robin dead. A novel, then, is not a short story made longer, but a short story made deeper.

TIPS AND TECHNIQUES

Don't let a novel's length put you off. It's often easier to write a novel than it is to write a good short story.

Now it's your turn

In a circle

If you are struggling with your story map, try this exercise.

1. Sketch your hero inside a circle in the center of a piece of paper. As you draw, imagine that you are that hero, deciding which way to go. Think about the problems he or she has and what might be done about them.

2. Draw six spokes around your hero circle. Each leads to another circle. Inside each one, sketch a different scene or write it as notes. Each circle will be a course of action that your hero might take or some obstacle in his or her path.

3. Give yourself 20 minutes and write down only your first thoughts.

You have planned your plot and are ready start your story. Focus on your hero. Now put on your hero's skin. Think about your problems as the hero. What is at stake? Where will you start the story?

Hooking your readers

Some stories jump right into a dramatic scene, then backtrack shortly afterward to explain things to readers. Others start with a prologue, giving the story's historical context. You could also start with a brief scene set just before a crisis comes. This lets you show the hero's usual life just before a conflict makes it worse—just before a Viking invasion, for example. Your hero must then act or face the consequences.

Fast and furious

Karen Cushman's *Catherine, Called Birdy* is about a teenager in a fury. The date is 1290, and the 14-year-old heroine, Catherine, a minor lord's daughter, has been ordered by her older brother to keep a diary. From the first lines, we are hooked:

> **12TH DAY OF SEPTEMBER**
> I am commanded to write an accou of my days: I am bit by fleas and plagued by family. This is all there is to say.
>
> **13TH DAY OF SEPTEMBER**
> My father must suffer from ale head this day, for he whacked me twice before dinner instead of once. I hope his angry liver bursts.
>
> **14TH DAY OF SEPTEMBER**
> Tangled my spinning again. Corpus bones, what a torture.

High tension

V. A. Richardson's *The House of Windjammer* starts with a shipwreck and the loss of a family fortune. From the first lines, we know things will only get worse for the family:

> *They were lost. All aboard the Sirius knew it now. Lucien Windjammer cursed under his breath. The Sirius rode uneasily on the swell, moving through the fog like a ghost ship.*
> V. A. Richardson, *The House of Windjammer*

Bizarre beginnings

In *Daughter of Venice*, Donna Jo Napoli uses names and objects that are common to the location and time period to introduce the setting and make the reader want to learn more.

> *The Canal Grande is busy. That's nothing new to us. From our bedchamber balcony my sisters and I watch the daily activity. Our palazzo stands on the Canal Grande and our rooms are three flights up, so we have a perfect view. But down here in the gondola, with the noise of the boats, and the smell of the sea, and the glare of the sun on the water, not even the thin gauze of my veil can mute the bold lines of this delightful chaos.*
>
> Donna Jo Napoli, *Daughter of Venice*

TIPS AND TECHNIQUES

Study lots of opening sentences. Decide which ones work best and why. Make your own opening mysterious, dramatic, or funny. Write it and rewrite it. Introduce the conflict in the first line, or soon afterward. Send your heroes dramatically on their way.

Stories often falter after an exciting opening, so be sure to build interest and add complication. It is important to find ways to crank up the tension.

Add some action

Keep your characters active at all times— battles, chases, runaway horses, shipwrecks, etc. But be sure the action arises from your characters' plans, and not your need to add excitement. In the excerpt below, see how Crispin gets caught outside and trapped in an alley by men who mean to harm him:

> *Gulping for breath, I halted and spun about, only to find that another man had come up behind me. I flung myself against a wall, even as I struggled to get Bear's dagger out of my pocket. With the two men keeping to either side of me, I was unable to confront them both. But one, I saw, had a large stick in his hand. The other held a knife. "Keep away!" I screamed, finally managing to pull Bear's dagger free from its sheath.*
> Avi, *Crispin: The Cross of Lead*

Character conflict

Supporting characters can add intrigue and suspense. In V. A. Richardson's *The House of Windjammer*, Jade tries to help Adam. However, because she is his enemy's daughter, Adam suspects her at every turn. This puts both of them in danger.

TIPS AND TECHNIQUES

If the middle of your story seems thin, pile on the challenges for your heroes—make their lives miserable. If you run out of ideas, look through your research notes.

False happy endings

These can be useful partway through a story. In *Catherine, Called Birdy*, by Karen Cushman, Birdy's father decides to marry her off to restore the family fortunes. There is a false happy ending when the heroine succeeds in driving away the first suitor. But then her father comes up with another— maintaining the readers' interest and building tension.

Explore your hero's weaknesses

Your hero's weaknesses can add suspense to a tough situation. In Leon Garfield's *The Empty Sleeve*, Peter Gannet lets his ambition lead him into dangerous situations. He soon learns that keys are valuable items and can earn him the money he needs to pay for his passage on a ship. But will his employer find out?

> *For an alarming instant, as he fumbled for the key behind the mirror, he was glared at by his own reflection; and was shocked by how young and frightened he looked. Shakily he got hold of the key and crept down the stairs with it.*
>
> Leon Garfield, *The Empty Sleeve*

Build stories upon stories

In The Orphan Train Adventures series by Joan Lowery Nixon, the Kelly children are sent on the Orphan Train by their poor, widowed mother to find families who can give them a good life. Each book follows the different Kelly children as they are adopted and brought to their new homes. Frances dresses as a boy to protect her brother. Mike runs away to join the Army. Danny plots to reunite his family. Megan thinks she is cursed by a gypsy. As soon as one book ends, another begins. Will the entire Kelly family ever be settled?

S tories build in suspense until they reach a climax. After this, the heroes' main problems will be solved. If they go back to their old lives, they will have learned something, conquered an enemy, or overcome a weakness.

The climax

In an action story, the climax is likely to be some kind of battle with the main enemy. The enemy might be a person or it might be the learning of a painful truth that sets the hero on a new course and ends the story on a hopeful note.

Counting the cost

Heroes may pay a price for winning in the end. They could lose a friend, a cherished hope, or a valued possession. At the very least, they will be older, and some of their youthful innocence will be lost.

TIPS AND TECHNIQUES

Good endings usually link to the beginning. This reminds readers of how much the hero has changed in the course of the story and how much has happened.

Now it's your turn

Choose your own ending

Read the ending of your favorite historical-fiction book. Decide what you liked about it and what you didn't. Write your own ending. Put it aside and read it later. Do you still think your ending is better?

Endings suggest a new beginning

Most readers like happy endings of some sort, but don't be predictable. In historical fiction, a typical fairy-tale ending won't be believable. Instead, focus on what the hero has gained from his or her experience. The hero may have been hurt but now has a chance to do better and have a good life.

Elizabeth George Speare's ending to *The Sign of the Beaver* suggests more adventures for Matt in the future:

> *Matt thrust his arms into his new jacket ... the cabin glowed, warm and filled with life. ... They would all sit together around the table and bow their heads while his father asked the blessing. Then he would tell them about Attean.*
> Elizabeth George Speare,
> *The Sign of the Beaver*

Bad endings

Bad endings are those that:
- fizzle out if you've run out of ideas
- have historically impossible solutions
- are too good to be true
- are too grim and leave the readers with no hope

MAKE YOUR WORDS WORK

In historical stories, every word must work hard to transport readers back in time. Pick the most telling details to bring the past to life.

Use sharp focus

Choose a few, precise details to create a scene. See how Geraldine McCaughrean describes pioneers stepping off the train in *Stop the Train*:

> *There was a middle-aged man in overalls and a woman's broad-brimmed straw hat. ... There was a widow in black, with a net purse swinging from her wrist, a knitting bag and a goat.*
> Geraldine McCaughrean, *Stop the Train*

Choose your words

Use powerful verbs. Sunlight may "reflect" off a drawn sword. But if it "glances," the verb could suggest a blade slashing in battle.

Now it's your turn

Wise words

Pick a word from a favorite book and, with a friend, take turns to see how many similar words you can come up with. Or pick a new word from the dictionary every day. Find ways to use it—make it part of a poem or brief story.

Use vivid imagery

In *The Empty Sleeve,* Leon Garfield uses striking similes: A snowstorm is "like a madman made of feathers" and "church steeples were as stiff and white as dead men's fingers." These images foreshadow bad things to come.

Change the rhythm and length of your sentences

Use short, punchy sentences when describing specific actions.

If something scary is going to happen, use longer sentences to build suspense.

Here is Peter Gannet being haunted by the whispers of ghostly apprentices, and that's only the start:

> *The whispering stopped. ... Then, suddenly, and with a violent rush, the door burst open! Instantly an icy wind rushed in, tore at the candle flame and put it out. Then silence returned. There was someone standing in the doorway ... a figure all in black, hooded and without a face.*
> Leon Garfield, *The Empty Sleeve*

Change the mood

Serious stories need lighter moments to make difficult scenes bearable or to distract readers before something really nasty happens. Humorous stories also need dashes of drama to hold readers' interest.

USE DRAMATIC DIALOGUE

Creating good dialogue is one of the biggest challenges for the historical-story writer. When it's right, it can add color, pace, mood, and suspense to your story.

Let your characters speak

Readers do not want to struggle with writers' attempts at medieval dialogue. When in doubt, opt for plain English that omits current expressions. (Look back at the excerpt from *Catherine, Called Birdy* on page 34. Karen Cushman uses authentic phrases like "corpus bones" and "ale head." But overall the diary is written in understandable English.)

Study other historical-fiction writers

People often spoke more formally in the past, and people of a lower class would have spoken respectfully to the upper classes. Listen to dialogue in historical TV dramas. Old letters can also give us a real sense of the past.

Eavesdrop

Listening to how people around you speak will show you how information flows back and forth between speakers. Notice that people often start mid-sentence or break off without finishing a sentence or thought.

GETTING STARTED   SETTING THE SCENE   CHARACTERS   VIEWPOINT

Now it's your turn

Family chat

Spend 10 minutes writing down how your family talks at home. Include all the hesitations and repetitions. Compare your notes to some dialogue in a book. You will see at once that it does not include all the hesitations of natural speech. Fictional dialogue gives an edited impression of real speech.

Following convention

The way dialogue is written follows certain conventions, or rules. It is usual to start a new paragraph for every new speaker. What the speaker says is enclosed in quotation marks, followed by speech tags ("she said," "he said," or "she asked") to show who's speaking.

> *"Grandma says your dad ain't got the sticking power of a monkey on a greased pole."*
>
> *"Excuse me!" retorted Cissy. "I don't know that someone who ain't acquainted with some other person ought to go bandying monkeys...!"*
>
> Geraldine McCaughrean, *Stop the Train*

USE DRAMATIC DIALOGUE

If you need to give readers details of a character's actions or history, it's often quicker and more interesting to do it in a conversation. If characters discuss or argue about something in the past, readers learn lots about them and their history.

Information as conversation

Here's an example from *Carrie's War* by Nina Bawden. Auntie Lou tries to excuse the behavior of her brother, Mr. Evans:

> *"Oh, his bark's worse than his bite. Though he won't stand to be crossed, so don't be too cheeky and mind what he says. I've always minded him—he's so much older, you see."*
>
> Nina Bawden, *Carrie's War*

A sense of doom

In Leon Garfield's *The Empty Sleeve*, Mr. Bagley, the old ship's carpenter, predicts troubles ahead for the Gannet twins:

> *"I done the best I could for your boys, Mr. G," confided the old man, earnestly. "I rigged their vessels under tops'ls only. That way they'll ride out the squalls. ... It's best to be prepared for the worst, Mr. G, for them squalls has got to come. Most of all, for young Peter here. Saturday's child, born on the chime, will surely see ghosts..."*
>
> Leon Garfield, *The Empty Sleeve*

Now it's your turn

The art of communication

Write another descriptive line of dialogue about Mr. Evans based on Auntie Lou's account of him on the previous page. Indicate her feelings about her brother. These are only suggested by what she says, but they are quite important. Think about how a few words of dialogue tell a lot about a character. Once finished, compare your version to the original.

Create tension

Dialogue can be used to create different atmospheres—mysterious, humorous, tragic, or happy. It can be used to build tension and foreshadow dangers ahead. In this excerpt, Adam Windjammer has been waylaid by street boys. Note the sense of menace conjured up by the writer:

"Looks like a rich boy, Wolfie," one said. "Shut your m-mouth, can't you!" the hungry-looking youth stammered... "How many t-times have I told you not to use my name when we're r-robbing?"

"Robbing!" Adam gasped. "But I don't have any money."

"Is that the t-truth of it?" Wolfie said. "Well, we'll be the j-judge of that."

V. A. Richardson,
The House of Windjammer

TIPS AND TECHNIQUES

Avoid idle chatter. If any piece of dialogue doesn't advance your story, cut it out.

USE DRAMATIC DIALOGUE

Good dialogue can reveal what characters are really like. Speech patterns can show social status, education, regional origins, and age, as well as suggesting the historical period.

Class difference

In *The Empty Sleeve*, Leon Garfield uses modern English while showing 18th-century class differences in the ways characters address one another. Here, the young locksmith's apprentice Peter Gannet meets Lord Marriner in the local tavern. The aristocrat calls Peter only by his master's name. In return, Peter uses a formal address and speaks rather nervously, as the stammered "y-yes" hints.

> *"You're Mr. Woodcock's boy, aren't you?" said his lordship, kindly.*
> *"Y-yes, your lordship."*
> *The waiter returned with the port.*
> *"Your health, Mr. Woodcock's boy!"*
>
> Leon Garfield, *The Empty Sleeve*

Regional accents

Used with care, bits of regional speech—turns of phrase and accents—can enrich the characters and make the time and place of the story seem real. The characters in *The Sign of the Beaver* are pioneer settlers in Maine in the 1770s. Elizabeth George Speare makes this apparent through the dialogue and the old-fashioned words, such as "reckon."

> *"Six weeks," his father had said that morning.*
> *"Maybe seven. Hard to reckon exactly."*
>
> Elizabeth George Speare, *The Sign of the Beaver*

GETTING STARTED   SETTING THE SCENE   CHARACTERS   VIEWPOINT

Suggest the past

Caroline Lawrence's The Roman Mysteries series has four very different main characters from Roman times: Flavia, an aristocrat; Jonathan, an outspoken Jewish doctor's son; Nubia, a freed African slave who struggles to speak formal Latin; and Lupus, a mute ex-street boy. The writer adds occasional words or phrases to suggest the period and the characters' backgrounds.

> *"Doctor Mordecai!" gasped Flavia.*
> *"You look just like a Roman."*
> *"Behold!" said Nubia. "You have cut your hairs."*
> *With his forefinger, Lupus pretended to shave his own smooth cheeks.*
> *"And shaved off your beard!" agreed Jonathan. "Great Jupiter's eyebrows, father! Why did you do that?"*
>
> Caroline Lawrence,
> The Roman Mysteries

Reveal education

The Seeing Stone is set in 12th-century England, just before the fourth Crusade. The quest for Jerusalem is on everyone's minds. Here, Gatty, a servant girl, shows her lack of education by asking Arthur, a scholarly lord's son, if Jerusalem is farther away than the nearby English city of Chester:

> *"Much, much farther," I said.*
> *"Why?"*
> *"Why's because I want to see where Jesus was born. Instead of Ludlow fair, let's go to Jerusalem."*
> *"Gatty!" I said. "You can't walk to Jerusalem."*
> *"I can and all," said Gatty.*
> *"You can't," I said. "Only a magician could. It's across the sea."*
> *Gatty lowered her head and looked at the ground. "I didn't know that," she said.*
>
> Kevin Crossley-Holland, *The Seeing Stone*

Now it's your turn

Who's who?

Choose two characters from historical fiction who are different from each other in a particular way—perhaps one is richer, more educated, or from a different place or social class. Invent a conversation between them. Think of ways to show their differences—both in their choice of words and in what they say. Take your time; get it just right.

BEAT WRITER'S BLOCK

Sometimes even the best writers can run out of words. This is called writer's block. It can last for days, but regular practice and lots of brainstorming will help. Here are some common causes:

Thinking what you have written is no good

Remember the story executioner—your internal critic that belittles your work? Well, give him the ax. Do some timed brainstorming at once: List the historical figures you'd most like to meet, your time machine's future destinations, how many words mean "old," and so on. Just get yourself writing again.

Thinking everyone else is a better writer

Even experienced writers fall into this trap. But remember, the more you practice, the more you will improve. You could use your skills to write for history magazines. Documenting the past is the biggest story of all!

Case study

The poet Samuel Taylor Coleridge had one of the first known cases of writer's block. In 1804 he wrote: "Yesterday was my Birth Day. So completely has a whole year passed, with scarcely the fruits of a month—O Sorrow and Shame. I have done nothing!"

Now it's your turn

Mystery time travel

In your next writing practice, imagine you are traveling in your time machine once more. It stops. The door opens. Step outside. Search for clues that tell you where you've landed. Are you pleased or petrified? Pour out your thoughts for 10 minutes.

No ideas

Thinking you have no ideas is a common block, but as a history lover, you will never run short of material. There are centuries' worth of stories waiting to be told. Visit your local museum, a national museum, or a favorite historic place. Go out and search for a story.

Rejection or external criticism

No one enjoys rejection or criticism, but it is an important part of learning to be a writer. If you invite someone to share your stories, be prepared for some negative comments. They may be more useful than flattery. See them as a reason to improve and rewrite your story if it really needs it.

If you are stuck mid-story, you may not have done enough planning. Do you know what your hero really wants? Ask yourself if your plot has left him or her stranded.

Ways to stir your imagination

"What if?" is a good question to ask if your story isn't quite clear. What if the hero is really a noble person's son but doesn't realize it? This is what happens in Charles Dickens' famous book *Oliver Twist*, where the boy is seemingly condemned to life in the workhouse.

Character forming

If you still don't know your hero well enough to work out his or her story, try this exercise. Write the heading "My Hero" on a sheet of paper. Divide the left margin into 10 squares, with the following headings in each one: looks; wears; lives in; feels; owns; is good at; is bad at; his or her weakness is; his or her friends are; and his or her enemies are. For each category, take five minutes to write five thoughts. When you have finished, you will know 50 things about your hero.

Keep a diary

If you keep a journal, you should never stop writing. When you visit museums and other historic places, be sure to record all your thoughts and impressions. These could provide valuable research ideas. Make sure you read what you have written regularly.

Brainstorm with friends

Writing can be a lonely business. If your key character isn't coming to life, brainstorm with friends. Sit in a circle. Start by telling them a brief outline of your character's situation and who he or she is. Then let everyone ask you questions or make suggestions about what will happen next. It may help you to solve a serious plot problem.

Breaking down resistance

If you really are stuck with your writing, try telling someone else's story. Retell a local legend or use the *Robin Hood* synopsis on page 32 to write your own version of that story. The main thing is to finish it. Completing a piece of storytelling like this will spur you on with your own tales. Prove that you can finish something.

TIPS AND TECHNIQUES

Staring at a blank page waiting for inspiration to strike will only give you a headache and make you feel bad about yourself. Brainstorm a list. Write something. Something can always be improved. Nothing can't.

TAKE THE NEXT STEP

THE END

Completing your first story is a wonderful achievement. You have started to master your writer's craft and probably learned a lot about yourself, too. But now, you must seek out another quest. Put your first story away in your desk drawer and start a new tale.

Another story?

If you did a lot of research for your first story, the chances are you will already have enough material to write another. Perhaps, while you were writing, some other character's story drew your interest. See if there's an angle for another story.

How about a sequel to your first story?

Is there more to tell about the characters you have already created? Can you write a sequel that says what happens next? Celia Rees continued one of her stories when she wrote *Sorceress* as the sequel to *Witch Child*. Perhaps your hero is ready for another adventure, or maybe your novel features a minor character who deserves his or her own story.

What about a trilogy?

A trilogy usually covers one main story, split over three volumes. V. A. Richardson's *The House of Windjammer* and Kevin Crossley-Holland's Arthur books are trilogies. The hero's main problems are revealed in the first book, expanded in the second, and resolved in the third.

Or a quartet?

Joan Lowery Nixon wrote four books in The Orphan Train Adventures. The writer was inspired by tragic real-life events in 19th-century America when poor East Coast families were forced to send their children to the West on the orphan trains, hoping they would be adopted by pioneering families who could give them a better life.

Search the archives

Keep looking for stories: Visit museums, look through history books, learn about a specific invention, read the diary of a real historical figure, or nag a grandparent for more family stories. Joan Lowery Nixon got the idea for her stories this way. She says she wanted to "bring history and fiction together in an exciting, adventurous time and place, to tell the stories of those who could have traveled west on the orphan train."

Storytelling is a special skill, and success will not come overnight. Most well-known writers worked for years before publishing, and few authors make a living from writing. It is something people do for reasons other than money and fame.

So why do writers write?

- They write because they must.

- They write to tell a story that must be told.

- They write because they believe that nothing is more important than stories.

- They write because it's the thing they most want to do.

Celia Rees

Celia Rees (right), author of *Witch Child*, realized that the skills that condemned a woman to death in 17th-century Europe were valued among American Indians. What if a girl could move between those two societies? She said:

Writing a book, any book, is like taking a journey. You know the starting point, and (more or less) where you are heading, but you have no way of knowing exactly what is going to happen in between.

Rosemary Sutcliff

Rosemary Sutcliff, author of *Tristan and Iseult,* was born in England but spent her early life in Malta. She wrote 46 novels for young people. She was a sickly child and was home-schooled, and it was during this time that her mother read her the Celtic and Saxon legends that were to fire her love of history.

Elaine Marie Alphin

Elaine Marie Alphin (right), author of *Ghost Soldier*, wanted to be a paleontologist when she grew up, but writing became her great love. She says she writes "to make sense of my life, and out of the world around me. I write to explore new ideas."

Karen Cushman

Karen Cushman (below), author of *Catherine, Called Birdy*, didn't start writing books professionally until she was 50 years old. She especially liked the Middle Ages because big changes were happening in the way people looked and behaved, and how they thought about their own identity. These have connections with issues that young people face today. She says:

> My ideas come from reading and listening and living; they come
> from making mistakes and figuring things out. Ideas come
> from wondering a lot—such as what would happen
> if ... ? And then what would happen next?

PREPARE YOUR WORK

After your story has been resting in your desk for a month, take it out and read through it. You will be able to see your work with fresh eyes and spot strengths and flaws easily.

Edit your work

Reading your work aloud will help you to simplify rambling sentences and correct dialogue that doesn't flow. Cut out all unnecessary adjectives and adverbs, and extra words like "very" and "really." This will instantly make your writing crisper. Once you have cut down the number of words, decide how well the story works. Does it have a satisfying end? Has your hero resolved the conflict in the best possible way? When your story is as good as can be, write it out again or type it up on a computer. This is your manuscript.

Think of an exciting title

It is important to think of a good title—something intriguing and eye-catching. Think about some titles you know and like.

Be professional

If you have a computer, you can type up your manuscript and give it a professional presentation. Manuscripts should always be printed on one side of white paper, with wide margins and double spacing. Pages should be numbered, and new chapters should start on a new page. You can also include your title as a header on the top of each page. At the front, you should have a title page with your name, address, telephone number, and e-mail address on it. Repeat this information on the last page.

Make your own book

If your school has its own computer lab, why not use it to publish your own story or to make a story anthology (collection) with your friends. A computer will let you choose your own font (print style) or justify the text (making even margins like a professionally printed page). When you have typed and saved your story to a file, you can edit it quickly with the spelling and grammar checker, or move sections of your story around using the cut-and-paste tool, which saves a lot of rewriting. Having your story on a computer file also means you can print a copy whenever you need one, or revise the whole story if you want to.

Design a cover

Once your story is in good shape, you can print it out and use the computer to design the cover. A graphics program will let you scan and print your own artwork, or download ready-made graphics. Or you could use your own digital photographs and learn how to manipulate them on-screen to produce some highly original images. You can use yourself or friends as models for your story's heroes.

TIPS AND TECHNIQUES

Whether you write your story on a computer or by hand, always make a copy before you give it to others to read. Otherwise, if they lose it, you will have lost all your precious work.

REACH YOUR AUDIENCE

The next step is to find an audience for your historical fiction, whether it's a novel or a short story. Family members or classmates may be receptive. Or you may want to share your work through a Web site, magazine, or publisher.

Some places to publish your story

There are several magazines and a number of writing Web sites that accept stories and novel chapters from young writers. Some give writing advice. Several run regular competitions. Each site has its own rules about submitting work, so make sure you read them carefully before you send in a story. You can also:

• Send stories to your school's magazine. If your school doesn't have a magazine, start your own with like-minded friends.

• Keep your eyes peeled when reading your local newspaper or magazines. They might be running writing competitions you could enter.

• Check with local museums and colleges. Some run creative-writing workshops during school holidays.

Writing clubs

Starting a writing club or workshop group and exchanging stories is a great way of getting your historical-fiction story out there. It will also get you used to criticism from others, which will prove invaluable in learning how to write. Your local library might be kind enough to provide a space for such a club.

Finding a book publisher

Study the market and find out which publishers are most likely to publish historical fiction. Addresses of publishers and information about whether they accept submissions can be found in writers' handbooks at your local

library. Bear in mind that manuscripts that haven't been asked for or paid for by a publisher—unsolicited submissions—are rarely published. Secure any submission with a staple or paperclip and always enclose a short letter (explaining what you have sent) and a stamped, self-addressed envelope for the story's return.

Writer's tip

If your story is rejected by an editor, see it as a chance to make it better. Try again, and remember that having your work published is wonderful but it is not the only thing. Being able to make up a story is a gift, so why not give yours to someone you love? Read it to a younger brother or sister. Tell it to your grandmother. Find your audience.

Some final words

All good stories show us the truth about ourselves, even when they are about times long past. Historical fiction helps us to understand the past in different ways. But whether past or present, the best stories always explore the good and bad things that make us human. They show us new possibilities.

GLOSSARY

anachronism—something that is placed in the wrong historical time (such as a telescope in the hands of a Roman soldier)

analogy—a comparison that shows the resemblance between things in order to explain something clearly

antagonist—principal character in opposition to the protagonist or hero in fiction

chapter synopsis—an outline that describes briefly what happens in each chapter

cliffhanger—ending a chapter or scene of a story at a nail-biting moment

dramatic irony—when the reader knows something the characters don't

editing—removing all unnecessary words from your story, correcting errors, and rewriting the text until the story is the best it can be

editor—the person at a publishing house who finds new books to publish and advises authors on how to improve their stories by telling them what needs to be added or cut

first-person viewpoint—a viewpoint that allows a single character to tell the story as if he or she had written it; readers feel as if that character is talking directly to them; for example: "It was July when I left for Timbuktu. Just the thought of going back there made my heart sing."

foreshadowing—dropping hints of coming events or dangers that are essential to the outcome of the story

genre—a particular type of fiction, such as fantasy, historical, realistic, mystery, adventure, or science fiction

manuscript—your story when it is written down, either typed or by hand

metaphor—calling a man "a mouse" is a metaphor, a word picture; from it we learn in one word that the man is timid or weak, not that he is actually a mouse

motivation—the reason why a character does something

narrative—the telling of a story

omniscient viewpoint—an all-seeing narrator that sees all the characters and tells readers how they are acting and feeling

plot—the sequence of events that drive a story forward; the problems that the hero must resolve

point of view (POV)—the eyes through which a story is told

primary source—the term historians use to describe firsthand accounts written in the historical period they are studying, such as letters, diaries, or official documents like wills and marriage licenses

protagonist—the main character in a play or book

publisher—a person or company who pays for an author's manuscript to be printed as a book and who distributes and sells that book

sequel—a story that carries an existing one forward

simile—saying something is like something else, a word picture, such as "clouds like frayed lace"

synopsis—a short summary that describes what a story is about and introduces the main characters

theme—the main idea behind a story, such as overcoming a weakness, the importance of friendship, or good versus evil; a story can have more than one theme

third-person viewpoint—a viewpoint that describes the events of the story through a single character's eyes, such as "Jem's heart leapt in his throat. He'd been dreading this moment for months."

unsolicited submission—a manuscript that is sent to a publisher without being requested; these submissions usually end up in the "slush pile," where they may wait a long time to be read

writer's block—when writers think they can no longer write or have used up all their ideas

FURTHER INFORMATION

Visit your local libraries and make friends with the librarians. They can direct you to useful sources of information, including magazines that publish young people's short fiction. You can learn your craft and read great stories at the same time. Librarians will also know if any published authors are scheduled to speak in your area.

Many authors visit schools and offer writing workshops. Ask your teacher to invite a favorite author to speak at your school.

On the Web

For more information on writing *Historical Fiction*, use FactHound to track down Web sites related to this book.
1. Go to *www.facthound.com*
2. Type in a search word related to this book or this book ID: 0756516404
3. Click on the *Fetch It* button.
FactHound will find the best Web sites for you.

Read more historical fiction

Alphin, Elaine Marie. *Ghost Soldier.* New York: Henry Holt, 2001.

Bawden, Nina. *Carrie's War.* Philadelphia: Lippincott, 1973.

Crossley-Holland, Kevin. *The Seeing Stone.* New York: Arthur A. Levine Books, 2001.

Curtis, Christopher Paul. *The Watsons Go to Burmingham.* New York: Delacorte Press, 1995.

Cushman, Karen. *Catherine, Called Birdy.* New York: Clarion Books, 1994.

Donnelly, Jennifer. *A Northern Light.* San Diego: Harcourt, Inc., 2003.

Erdrich, Louise. *The Birchbark House.* New York: Hyperion Books for Children, 1999.

Giff, Patricia Reilly. *Lily's Crossing.* New York: Delacorte Press, 1997.

Lowry, Lois. *Number the Stars.* Boston: Houghton Mifflin Co., 1989.

McCaughrean, Geraldine. *Stop the Train.* New York: HarperCollins, 2003.

Napoli, Donna Jo. *Daughter of Venice.* New York: Delacorte Press, 2002.

Park, Linda Sue. *A Single Shard.* New York: Clarion Books, 2001.

Pfitsch, Patricia Curtis. *Riding the Flume.* New York: Simon & Schuster Books for Young Readers, 2002.

Rees, Celia. *Witch Child.* Cambridge, Mass.: Candlewick Press, 2001.

Salisbury, Graham. *Under the Blood-Red Sun.* New York: Delacorte Press, 1994.

Smucker, Barbara Claassen. *Runaway to Freedom: A Story of the Underground Railway.* New York: Harper & Row, 1978.

Taylor, Mildred D. *Roll of Thunder, Hear My Cry.* New York: Dial Press, 1976.

Walsh, Jill Paton. *A Parcel of Patterns.* New York: Farrar, Straus, and Giroux, 1983.

Westall, Robert. *The Machine Gunners.* New York: Greenwillow Books, 1976.

Whelan, Gloria. *Homeless Bird.* New York: HarperCollins, 2000.

Read all the Write Your Own books:

Write Your Own Adventure Story
ISBN: 0-7565-1638-2

Write Your Own Fantasy Story
ISBN: 0-7565-1639-0

Write Your Own Historical Fiction Story
ISBN: 0-7565-1640-4

Write Your Own Mystery Story
ISBN: 0-7565-1641-2

Write Your Own Realistic Fiction Story
ISBN: 0-7565-1642-0

Write Your Own Science Fiction Story
ISBN: 0-7565-1643-9

INDEX